Novels for Students, Volume 31

Project Editor: Sara Constantakis Rights Acquisition and Management: Jennifer Altschul, Margaret Chamberlain-Gaston, Leitha Etheridge-Sims, Kelly Quin Composition: Evi Abou-El-Seoud Manufacturing: Drew Kalasky

Imaging: John Watkins

Product Design: Pamela A. E. Galbreath, Jennifer Wahi Content Conversion: Katrina Coach Product Manager: Meggin Condino © 2010 Gale, Cengage Learning

For product information and technology assistance, contact us at **Gale Customer Support, 1-800-877-4253.**

For permission to use material from this text or product, submit all requests online at **www.cengage.com/permissions.**

Further permissions questions can be emailed to **permissionrequest@cengage.com** While every effort has been made to ensure the reliability of the information presented in this publication, Gale, a part of Cengage Learning, does not guarantee the accuracy of the data contained herein. Gale accepts no payment for listing; and inclusion in the publication of any organization, agency, institution, publication, service, or individual does not imply endorsement of the editors or publisher. Errors brought to the attention of the publisher and verified to the satisfaction of the publisher will be corrected in future editions.

Gale
27500 Drake Rd.
Farmington Hills, MI, 48331-3535

ISBN-13: 978-1-4144-4169-6
ISBN-10: 1-4144-4169-X
ISSN 1094-3552

This title is also available as an e-book.
ISBN-13: 978-1-4144-4947-0
ISBN-10: 1-4144-4947-X
Contact your Gale, a part of Cengage Learning sales
representative for ordering information.

Printed in the United States of America
1 2 3 4 5 6 7 14 13 12 11 10

Speak

Laurie Halse Anderson

1999

Introduction

Melinda Sordino is about to begin her first day of senior high school in Laurie Halse Anderson's 1999 novel *Speak*. Melinda cowers on the bus as she sits alone. She refers to herself as an outcast while she stands in the gym during freshman orientation. She sees her friends from middle school, and they see her. But no one speaks to her. When they laugh, Melinda senses they are laughing at her. Her ex-friends do not know what happened to her the night of the summer party. All they know is that Melinda ruined the party and got many of them in trouble when she called the police.

Melinda's experience is revealed very slowly in Anderson's provocative and touching novel. The book has won the praise of educators and critics for Anderson's ability to tell a disturbing story with irony, humor, and frankness. *Speak* was named a 2000 Printz Honor Book and was a finalist for both the 1999 National Book Award and Edgar Allan Poe Award.

In a voice that is well tuned to high school life in the 1990s, Anderson has created a character whose first year at Merryweather High is anything but merry. Melinda is psychologically tortured by her memories of having been raped. Those memories, which she refers to as the beast, lock her voice inside of her. She has no one she can trust to share her story with. When she finally gains the courage to speak, her ex-best friend calls her a liar. The only person who knows about that night is the student who raped her. It is not until he tries to do it again that Melinda finds the strength to speak and to stop him.

Anderson was born on October 23, 1961, in Potsdam, New York. After high school, Anderson attended Onondaga Community College in Syracuse, New York, the setting of her novel. Later she transferred to Georgetown University in Washington, D.C., where she earned a bachelor's degree in languages and linguistics.

From 1989 until 1992, Anderson worked as a reporter for two newspapers in Philadelphia, the *Record* and the *Inquirer*. Between 1992 and 1998, she turned to freelancing, writing articles for various trade journals. Later, she decided to write children's books and has not turned back since. The first book she wrote was *Ndito Runs*, a picture book published in 1996. Her next two books, both featuring the same characters, were *Turkey Pox* (1996) and *No Time for Mother's Day* (1999).

Speak (1999) was Anderson's first young adult novel. Her 2002 novel *Catalyst* is set in the same high school as *Speak* and even contains some of the same characters. Anderson's more recent titles include *Wintergirls* (2009), about a girl suffering from anorexia, and *Chains* (2008), about the eighteenth-century lives of teenage slaves. The award-winning author's books frequently appear on the *New York Times Best Seller List*. Anderson stated in an interview with Julie Prince in *Teacher Librarian*, "I've never worried about trends or trying to catch the next big thing. I write the stories that I can hear in my heart. It seems to be an effective strategy." Anderson then added, "I had my own struggles as an adolescent and I remember what it feels like to be lost and overwhelmed."

After college, the author married Greg Anderson. The couple had two daughters. The Andersons later divorced. She has since married Scot Larrabee and lives in upper state New York. Anderson writes a blog called *Mad Woman in the Forest* at http://halseanderson.livejournal.com to keep her reader fans up-to-date on her travels as she journeys around the nation on speaking tours.

Plot Summary

First Marking Period

Anderson's novel *Speak* begins with the protagonist, Melinda Sordino, on her way to the first day of high school. Melinda is very nervous about boarding the bus, though the reason for her tension is not provided. The school bus is empty when she gets on, but she carefully contemplates where she will sit. Although sitting in the front of the bus reminds her of being in elementary school, she decides sitting close to the front door is her best choice. By the time the bus arrives at school, Melinda is the only student who sits alone. All her old friends have shunned her.

Inside the school gym, Melinda looks to find someone to stand with. She recognizes the different groups by types, such as the athletes, the cheerleaders, the Plain Janes. Her middle-school friends look her way and laugh. Melinda assumes they are laughing at her. No one motions for her to join them. When she spots Rachel Bruin, who used to be her best friend, Melinda sees Rachel mouth the words "I hate you." Melinda turns away and remains in her group of one. She names her group the Outcast.

Melinda wanders from class to class, offering a cynical view of her teachers. Her English teacher is dubbed Hairwoman, because of the woman's long black hair that is tinged in neon orange at the tips. Melinda refers to her social studies teacher as Mr. Neck, because of the thickness of his neck. Mr. Freeman, her art teacher, retains his name. He makes her feel relaxed and appears, to Melinda, to be more sane than most other adults in her life. Mr. Freeman tells his students that in his class they will discover their souls. For their first assignment, students pull pieces of paper out of an old globe. On the papers are names of objects. Melinda's paper contains the word *tree*. Mr. Freeman says that they will use this object as their model for all the art work they will complete that year. They may paint, sketch, sculpt, or use any other medium they choose. However, all their work will focus on their selected object. Their grades will be based on how well they express an emotion through their finished pieces.

Later, Melinda thinks about her mother, with whom she has a strained relationship. Her mother manages a clothing store in downtown Syracuse. Most clothing stores that Melinda is familiar with and where her friends shop are located in the suburban malls. Downtown stores are considered dangerous. Melinda believes her mother likes the challenge. Her mother thrives on doing things that scare other people. Melinda demonstrates, as the novel progresses, that, unlike her mother, her most dominant emotion is fear.

The only student willing to associate with Melinda is a new girl named Heather. She is very unlike Melinda. She is very attentive to her clothes and her grooming, wants to be popular, and seeks ways to insert herself in the middle of school activities. Heather dominates Melinda, telling her how and what to eat at lunchtime and criticizing Melinda's negative outlook about socializing, exercising, and attending classes. However, Heather is better than nothing. Melinda goes along with Heather's plans and accepts her evaluations because Melinda also feels that having at least one friend is better than being alone.

One day, while Melinda is attempting to avoid Mr. Neck, who is trailing her because she has not turned in her assignments, Melinda ducks into a janitor closet to hide. In the back of the closet she discovers an overstuffed chair and decides this will be the perfect place to get away if the pressure of school becomes too intense. Eventually, she hangs up posters and some of her art projects, claiming the space as her personal lounge.

At a pep rally before a football game, a student Melinda does not know asks, "Aren't you the one who called the cops at Kyle Rodgers's party?" Another student adds, "My brother got arrested at that party." Then the student says, "I can't believe you did that." It is through these statements that readers gain further insights into Melinda's social problems.

Melinda receives her report card, and her parents explode. She gets an A in art, a B in biology, and Cs in everything else. Previously, she received straight As.

Media Adaptations

- In 2003, *Speak* was adapted to film, starring Kristen Stewart as Melinda. The movie was produced by Speak Film Inc., and directed by Jessica Sharzer. The film was released as a DVD in 2005.

- *Speak* is available on CD, read by Mandy Siegfried, at audiobooks.com and published in 2008 by Listening Library.

Second Marking Period

Melinda begins to show physical symptoms of her stress. She chews on her lips hard enough to draw blood and scabs have formed around her mouth. Her throat is always sore, which she believes is from having to hold back screams. She says she has a beast that is locked inside her. The beast represents the memories of what happened to her on the night of the summer party. She seldom speaks to anyone, even when they ask questions. Her thoughts are so disoriented that she cannot manage words. She has headaches and rarely sleeps.

In her biology class, David Petrakis sits next to her. Melinda believes that he has the potential to be cute one day. She also fantasizes about being friends with him. David is also in her social studies class. One day after Mr. Neck cuts off a spontaneous classroom debate about immigrants, David stands up to him and demands a right to speak. A few days later, David brings a video recorder to class to gather information about Mr. Neck's teaching performance. Rumors are that David is working to gather evidence for a suit against Mr. Neck. Melinda is impressed. David becomes her hero.

On Thanksgiving Day, Melinda's mother is called to the store on an emergency. So Melinda's father must cook the turkey. Her dad makes a mess and has to throw the turkey away. Melinda gets an idea to use the turkey bones for an art project. She rescues the carcass. Mr. Freeman is impressed with the sculpture that Melinda creates from the bones and other found objects. When Melinda finds a doll's head, she seals the doll's mouth with tape. From this, Mr. Freeman senses Melinda is in pain. When he acknowledges this, Melinda runs from the classroom.

On Christmas Day, Melinda is touched

emotionally when her parents give her art supplies. They have noticed she has taken an interest in drawing. The fact that they have noticed her is what impresses Melinda. This makes her want to tell them what happened to her, but she quickly changes her mind.

Back at school in her biology class, Melinda and her partner David must dissect a frog. David places the frog on its back and pins its feet to the dissecting board. Melinda raises the knife to make a cut down the length of the frog's belly when her mind is flooded with a flashback to that summer night. She hears a scream deep inside her and feels a pain. Then she passes out. As she falls, she hits her head against the table and must go to the hospital. As a doctor flashes a light into her eyes, checking for signs of a concussion, Melinda wonders if the doctor can see her thoughts. She wishes he could cut out all her memories.

A few days later, Andy Evans comes to the table where Melinda is sitting, eating her lunch. Some of Melinda's former friends are sitting at the other end. Andy stops behind Melinda and plays with her ponytail. She runs to the bathroom and pukes. Andy is the boy who raped her. It worries Melinda that her ex-best friend flirts with Andy.

Report cards come out. Melinda's grades are getting worse.

Third Marking Period

Melinda misses the school bus and must walk

to school. She passes a bakery. Just as she approaches the front door, Andy walks out. She freezes in fright. Andy asks if she wants a bite of his donut. She cannot speak, but she does run. As she escapes, she wonders why she did not run that summer night when he attacked her. Why did she stay and take his punishment?

In Hairwoman's English class, the students are reading *The Scarlet Letter*. The story is about a woman who has committed adultery and is forced to wear a red letter *A* on her chest. Melinda thinks that she and this woman would have been good friends. She thinks she should wear the letter *S* on her clothes. The *S* would stand for "silent, for stupid, for scared. S for silly. For shame."

The tree Melinda is working on in art class is frustrating her. She has tried to paint a tree, to sketch a tree, and to carve a tree out of a linoleum tile. None have worked.

Melinda's relationship with Heather is, at best, strained. Heather has joined a group called The Marthas. One of the rules of this group is that they buy similar clothes and wear coordinated outfits to school. They also do charitable work. Heather always enlists Melinda's help. Heather, being the newest member, is given all the grunt work, which she then passes on to Melinda. Melinda always caves in, as Heather is her only friend. At lunch one day, Heather tells Melinda that the two of them have nothing in common. She thanks Melinda for being nice to her when school first started, but it is now time to cut their ties. She also says Melinda is depressed and should seek help.

A white envelope is taped to Melinda's locker on Valentine's Day. She does not know how to react to it. She has a glimmer of hope that it might be from David, but she does not want to get too excited. The envelope could also be a cruel joke. So she does not open it right away. After her next class, she comes back to her locker and opens the envelope. It is from Heather. Besides the card, the friendship necklace that Melinda gave Heather is inside. Heather thanks Melinda for understanding. Melinda is crushed.

Mr. Freeman hands Melinda a book on the artist Pablo Picasso in art class. He thinks it will give her some ideas. After reading it, Melinda draws a tree in cubist form, with lots of geometric shapes. Mr. Freeman is impressed. After school, he sees Melinda walking toward town and offers a ride. Before he drops her off, he tells her he is available at any time if she needs to talk.

A few days later, Melinda runs into David at a basketball game. He invites her to a party at his house. She refuses the invitation. She is afraid that he might be lying about his parents being there. She thinks he might be luring her into a position where she cannot defend herself. She cannot stand the thought of his touching her. Later, she gets angry with herself for refusing to go. She then thinks back on the events of that summer party. She went with a group of her girlfriends. Most of the kids there were older and were drinking. Melinda drank beer for the first time in her life and got sick. She went outside, fearing she might vomit. Andy followed her. She was amazed that he paid attention to her. He pulled her into him and started kissing her. All she could think was how amazed her girlfriends would be if they could see her in Andy's arms. But things went too far, and Melinda struggled to get free. Andy covered her mouth with his hand and forced her to the ground. He hurt her. Then he left her lying there.

Melinda was only thirteen. She had no experience with other boys. She did not know what to do next. She could only think of calling the police. When they came, Melinda had run away. She did not want to tell anyone.

The third report card comes out. Melinda gets an A in art, but all the other grades are Ds and Fs.

Fourth Marking Period

Ivy is in Melinda's art class. Ivy is the first not to shun her. Ivy knows nothing of what happened at the summer party, but she appreciates the art projects that Melinda creates. She praises Melinda, telling her she is better than she realizes. She encourages Melinda when she shows signs of giving up. Ivy and Mr. Freeman help to rebuild Melinda's self-confidence.

When Melinda notices how attached Rachel is to Andy, she tries to warn her. She senses that she cannot come right out and tell her what happened, but she does send her an anonymous note telling Rachel to be careful. When Melinda's note to Rachel does not appear to affect her, Melinda finally tells Rachel that Andy raped her. Rachel is furious with Melinda, telling her she is just jealous because Andy has asked Rachel to the prom.

While at home, sick with the flu, Melinda again reflects on the summer party. It is the first time that she is able to see that she did nothing wrong. She did not entice Andy. She even told him to stop. She did not want to have sex with him. She was raped. Up until then she was too overcome with shame to acknowledge this. Now, as she is able to more fully grasp what actually happened, she knows that what Andy did was wrong.

Rachel breaks up with Andy. Apparently, Andy became too aggressive, and Rachel fought him off. Andy is furious about this. When he learns that Melinda warned Rachel, he follows Melinda to the janitor's closet and traps her. He is harsh with her both verbally and physically and tries to rape her again. This time, Melinda screams out and tries to push him away. She makes it out of the closet unscathed. At the end of the story, Melinda creates the perfect tree in art class, a tree that opens up all her emotions, and Melinda begins to tell Mr. Freeman what happened to her.

Characters

Rachel Bruin

Rachel was the protagonist's best friend from elementary school through middle school. She is the one person that Melinda wishes she could talk to. However, Rachel believes that Melinda ruined her summer because of the police raid on the last party before school resumed.

Rachel hangs out with foreign exchange students at school. She takes up the habit of pretending to smoke candy cigarettes to give her a more European flair. When Melinda runs into Rachel in the girls' bathroom, Rachel responds to Melinda's statements with grunts or foreign phrases. Melinda learns that Rachel changes the spelling and pronunciation of her name to Rachelle, to sound more French.

When Melinda sees Rachel falling for Andy, Melinda wants to warn her. Melinda finally gets up the courage to do so, but Rachel thinks Melinda is jealous. However, it is because of Melinda's warning that Rachel finally sees who Andy really is. When he becomes to sexually aggressive at the prom, Rachel is strong enough to resist him. There is no statement in the novel that Rachel and Melinda mend their relationship, but Melinda does notice that after the prom, Rachel has taken an interest in one of the male foreign exchange students, which

Melinda applauds.

Dad

Melinda has only a surface relationship with both her parents. However, she appears to be closer to her father. They have an unspoken understanding of one another, which usually means they leave one another alone. Melinda often comes home to an empty house, eats her dinner alone, and then retreats upstairs to her room. Later, when her father returns home, Melinda listens to the sounds he makes and tries to guess what he is doing, such as microwaving his dinner, pouring himself a drink, turning on the television. They seldom speak to one another. Melinda's attitude toward life, in many ways, mimics her father's style. This is exposed on Thanksgiving when after Melinda's mother must abandon dinner plans to go to work, her father throws the turkey in the trash after unsuccessful attempts at cooking it. They order pizza instead of eating the traditional meal, which pleases both of them. It appears that her father is only vaguely aware of who Melinda is, what she is doing with her life, and what she is feeling. Her father is oblivious to the signs of her depression.

Andy Evans

Andy Evans is a handsome, well dressed senior at Merryweather High School. Girls are very much aware of him and would give anything to go out with him. At least this is true in the beginning of the year, especially among the freshmen girls. Andy appears to enjoy hanging with the freshmen, and one can assume that he is preying on their innocence.

Melinda, in her secret thoughts, refers to Andy as *It*. She is very reluctant to say his name. Andy comes up to her, at one point in the story, and plays with her ponytail as he talks to some of the other freshmen girls. He appears unaware that he has done anything damaging to Melinda. He eventually latches on to Rachel, Melinda's ex-best friend. When he discovers that Melinda has told Rachel about what he did to her, Andy corners her in the janitor's closet. He tells her that she wanted to have sexual relations with him at that summer party and should not be spreading rumors otherwise. He then tries to force himself on Melinda again. When Melinda fights back, Andy gets angry. Melinda yells out for help and is able to escape from Andy. Nothing is said, however, about what happens to Andy after that. Readers are left in the dark in reference to whether Andy is punished for his crime.

Mr. Freeman

Mr. Freeman is an art teacher at Merryweather High School. Melinda initially describes Mr. Freeman as being ugly. He reminds her of a grasshopper or a circus entertainer walking on stilts. He has a big nose and talks a lot. As the story progresses, though, Mr. Freeman becomes

Melinda's favorite teacher. She cannot believe he can get away with teaching his class the way he does because it is so much fun. Mr. Freeman encourages his students to reach down deep inside of themselves to find secrets they have never before realized they possess.

Mr. Freeman is also a father figure for Melinda. Throughout the story, it is Mr. Freeman who notices that Melinda is troubled and attempts to get her to open up. He encourages her art and praises her for her attempts. He tells her that he is always available should she want to talk. When words fail Melinda, Mr. Freeman implies that her emotions can be expressed through her projects. At the end of the story, in the final lines, the author suggests that Melinda goes to Mr. Freeman and begins to tell him her story.

Hairwoman

Hairwoman is the nickname that Melinda gives to her English teacher. Hairwoman is so named because she uses her dark, long hair, whose ends are dyed bright orange, to hide behind. She seldom gives her students eye contact. When she talks to them, her head is often bowed toward her desk, or she is turned toward the blackboard or the flag.

Heather

Heather is a new student at Merryweather High School. When she finds Melinda sitting alone, she assumes that Melinda is also new at the school. Melinda describes Heather as having a mouth full of braces, being in good physical shape, and talking way too much. However, Melinda welcomes Heather's company, at first. It is better than standing alone.

Heather needs to set goals for her future life in school. Melinda tolerates Heather, which makes Heather believe that Melinda agrees with her. Heather chooses the best clubs at school and makes every effort to be accepted. She takes on projects that are too big for her and then drags Melinda in on them, insisting that Melinda do some of the dirty work. In the end, after Melinda refuses to do any more work for her, Heather comes to Melinda and says that their relationship is not working out and should end. They have little in common, Heather says, and besides, Melinda's attitude is too negative. Heather returns a friendship necklace Melinda gave her and thanks Melinda for being so understanding.

Ivy

Ivy was not one of Melinda's close friends in middle school, but they did hang out from time to time. When Melinda finds Ivy in her art class, she tries to make contact with her, but Ivy does not notice. It is not until Melinda brings to class her unusual sculpture made with turkey bones that Ivy takes an interest. Ivy praises Melinda for her creativity and tells her, when Melinda becomes frustrated with her projects, that she is a good artist and should continue with her work.

Melinda believes that Ivy is the better artist, and she remarks on Ivy's good personality, a trait that makes it easy for Melinda to like her. Ivy goes looking for Melinda one day when Melinda abruptly leaves class. She finds Melinda in the girls' bathroom. While there, Melinda opens up a little about her feelings about Andy. Ivy joins in the conversation, telling Melinda that she is disgusted about how Rachel is falling all over Andy. Melinda is impressed that Ivy has noted the flaws in Andy's personality. She is also moved that Ivy was concerned enough to come looking for her, making sure that Melinda was all right.

Ms. Keen

Ms. Keen is Melinda's biology teacher. Very little is said about this particular teacher except for the strange clothes she wears. Melinda does not complain very much about Ms. Keen's teaching methods or the subject matter. In other ways, Ms. Keen is a nondescript teacher whom Melinda does not despise.

Mother

Melinda's mother is just the opposite of her daughter. Melinda states that her mother not only is fearless, she goes out of her way to confront dangerous situations. Her mother manages a store downtown in a dangerous district. She is often called away from her family to confront ongoing challenges and thus is seldom home. Melinda's mother is different in other ways too. She wants Melinda to buy clothes that Melinda does not feel comfortable with. The two of them have little in common. Melinda's mother is so busy, she hardly notices that Melinda is in emotional pain. She thinks that Melinda is rebelling against some unknown cause. She does not understand why Melinda is so quiet and why she is doing so poorly at school. Her solution is punishment, which does not work. Melinda is impressed, though, when her mother buys her art supplies for Christmas. She is pleased that her mother at least took a little time to notice her.

Mr. Neck

Mr. Neck, so called because Melinda sees him as a jock with a neck thicker than his head, is her social studies teacher. Mr. Neck makes statements about how well he knows students. When he first sees Melinda, he dubs her a troublemaker and pursues her in the halls, handing out demerits and other punishments when she fails to turn in a pass. Melinda paints Mr. Neck as arrogant and hypocritical. She also praises her fellow student, David Petrakis, for standing up to Mr. Neck's hypocrisy in class.

Nicole

Nicole is briefly mentioned as another of

Melinda's former friends. Nicole is an excellent athlete, the opposite of Melinda. She is a star soccer player, looked up to by even the male athletes. Gym teachers praise Nicole for her gifts. Nicole is neutral as far as friendship with Melinda is concerned. She neither shuns her nor goes out of her way to communicate.

David Petrakis

David Petrakis shares a lab table with Melinda in biology class. He shows signs that he is unaffected by the gossip that surrounds Melinda. Meanwhile, Melinda sometimes finds herself daydreaming about David as a potential boyfriend. One day, David invites Melinda to a pizza party at his house. Melinda is flattered, but she is also frightened by the proposal. She refuses the invitation because she is concerned he might merely want to lure her into another bad situation in which she might not be able to defend herself. David thus portrays some of the difficulties that Melinda faces in developing future intimate male relationships. As the story progresses, David grows on Melinda. He becomes her hero after he stands up to Mr. Neck's insulting behavior.

Melinda Sordino

Melinda is the protagonist of this story. She was thirteen years old when she was sexually attacked at a summer party. She has kept this a secret from everyone, and it is eating her up inside.

All that her parents know about this is that Melinda has suddenly become very quiet and her interest in school has begun a huge downward spiral. Melinda's friends only know that Melinda was at the party and while there called the cops. This caused trouble for many of the students who were there. Many were underage drinkers. Some lost their jobs because of this. Now, everyone at school shuns her.

Melinda has kept the attack a secret because she is ashamed. She feels she brought it on herself, even though she tried to fight the boy off. Much of the story is told from inside Melinda's head. There is very little dialogue with friends or family. Melinda lives through her feelings of self-doubt and the forced isolation that her secret has brought on.

Melinda's grades disintegrate as she cannot focus on her schoolwork and often skips class. All her energies are focused on keeping her emotions from exploding out of her. An abandoned janitor's closet becomes her refuge when she senses she is losing control of her fears and anxieties. She often wishes she could talk to someone, but she does not know how to start. She fears that other people will think she is despicable. Her parents are always too busy. Her friends have made it clear they already hate her. In the end, she finds her voice. She is able to refuse Heather's demands. This gives her the courage to stand up to Andy when he tries a second attack. Then she is ready to talk, to tell someone what really happened that night.

Trauma and the Restorative Power of Speech

The trauma of the rape that Melinda experiences before Anderson's novel *Speak* even begins influences the entire story. Because of that trauma, Melinda's mental state continues to deteriorate as the story progresses. As she attempts to find, within herself as well as in the world around her, places in which to hide, she sinks deeper into silence. So many people disallow her a chance to reveal her inner fears, shame, and confusion. Her peers have already judged her and decide to ban her from their groups. Her parents do not have time or patience to encourage her to open up to them. Only Melinda's art teacher perceives that something is troubling her. He is the only one who understands that sometimes words are either too difficult or too inadequate to express the deepest emotions. However, he also understands that in order for Melinda to heal, she must find a way to articulate her feelings. That is why he encourages her to speak symbolically through an art form. It is through art, the author suggests, that Melinda begins to unravel all the emotions that have entangled her mind. By working on her art project, Melinda begins to understand that she has no reason to feel guilty for what happened to her. Once she clears her mind, she is then able to think more clearly and in the process she informs herself of the truth of the rape. When she begins to speak out, she realizes that her role in the rape was that of victim not that of perpetrator, and thus the healing begins.

Friendship

The theme of friendship runs throughout Anderson's novel *Speak*. It is as if the author were posing questions about what true friendship is. Melinda, the protagonist, was once a fairly popular young girl. She had maintained friendships from elementary and middle school. However, because of one incident, she appears to have lost every friend she ever had. It was a big incident, but even still, why did no one bother to ask her side of the story? Why did everyone turn on her with one ex-friend going so far as stating that she hated her?

With friendship playing such an important role in high school, the loss of it, as portrayed in this novel, is almost as tragic as the rape that Melinda suffered. Melinda has no one to talk to, no one to sit with at lunch, no one to help her unravel the consequences of the terrible crime committed against her. The character Heather steps in as a pseudofriend, but Melinda soon discovers that there is no authenticity involved. Heather, like Melinda, is lonesome. She is the new kid in town and finds that breaking in with a crowd is very difficult. Heather uses Melinda to develop her plan to become popular. When Heather believes she has succeeded, she tells Melinda the two of them have nothing in common. Later, Heather returns the friendship necklace that Melinda gave her, thus making the break very clear.

The closest Melinda comes to having a true friend is in her relationship with Ivy, who is in Melinda's art class. The development of their friendship signals a turning point in the story. It is with Ivy that Melinda begins to express her fear and hatred of Andy, the boy who raped her. Melinda's steps toward being David's friend show signs of developing, but she is fearful of the thought of him touching her because of the rape. It is easier for her to start a friendship with Mr. Freeman, her art teacher. He is safer, in Melinda's judgment, because he is like a father figure. It is with Mr. Freeman, at the very end of the story, that Melinda begins to open up. And with this her healing begins, signaling the possibility of new friendships.

Identity

Another important theme is that of identity. The author takes readers into the lives of teens who are developing a sense of who they are outside of definitions of who their parents and teachers believe them to be. There are many struggles in the process. These struggles are playfully exaggerated in the constant changing of the school's mascot. As the school board tries on various rallying names for the school, from hornets to blue devils, so too the high school students try on different definitions of themselves. Rachel changes the sound of her name to Rachelle, making her appear more European. Heather joins a club whose identity is established through its members wearing matching outfits.

Topics for Further Study

- Research cubism, especially as Pablo Picasso developed it through his paintings. At one point in Anderson's story, Melinda's creativity is reawakened by studying Picasso's art. She draws a tree reflecting the concepts of cubism. Imagine what that tree might have looked like. Produce several samples of your own, using various media, such as charcoal, oil paints, and linoleum tiles, as Melinda did. Display your artwork for your class to see and explain what cubism is.

- What are the legal standards established by the U.S. Equal Employment Opportunity Commission and the U.S. Supreme Court that define sexual harassment? After researching this on the Internet and in your library, take a survey of students at your school, asking them how they define sexual harassment. Are there gaps between what students know and what the law is? After compiling your results, create a presentation for your class. Be ready to present your facts as well as answer questions.

- Interview your school counselors, asking them for advice about what a student should do if she thinks she is the victim of date rape. Then create a script that will be turned into a short film with student actors playing the roles of victim and counselor. The aim of this film should be to educate students on how to avoid this situation as well as what they should do if they find themselves a victim.

- Read Heidi Ayarbe's novel *Freeze Frame* (2008) about a teenage boy who accidentally shoots his friend. Kyle Carroll is the protagonist of this story, and like Melinda in

Speak, Kyle is ostracized by his fellow students. Compare the two stories. How do the two authors depict the psychological struggles that each protagonist goes through? How do the protagonists deal with the challenges they experience? How are those challenges resolved? Present your findings in an essay.

Melinda's struggle for identity is more serious. She calls herself an outcast in the beginning of the story. She does this for two reasons. First, her friends have shunned her. More critically, Melinda has shunned herself. She is ashamed about what happened to her, believing that she was at fault. Because of this, she has a constant struggle to keep her real self buried deep inside of her. She does not want to consider how she truly feels because she believes she is a monster. She refers to her reactions to the rape as the beast. There once was the sweet girl, the good student, the young girl with a lot of friends. And then there was the rape. Melinda's former identity no longer exists. What identity she claims now is uncertain. She cannot think straight. She would rather hide. It is not so much that she is hiding from the truth of who she is, but rather that she is hiding because she does not know the truth. To protect herself, Melinda has become a blank.

The lack of identity that Melinda experiences is exposed in her relationship with Heather. Melinda knows she has nothing in common with Heather. She dislikes the chores that Heather continues to talk her into doing. But Heather gives Melinda a hint of identity, so she clings to her. It is not until Melinda finally gains the courage to say "No" to Heather that she begins to reclaim her real identity. After that step, Melinda knows she must warn her ex-best friend Rachel about Andy, a step that exposes what has happened to her. Finally, Melinda also realizes that Andy was the culprit in the rape. She has nothing to be ashamed of. Once she begins to reclaim her identity, she is able to tell the whole story to Mr. Freeman and thus begin to heal.

Alienation

Despite the silence Melinda displays by either never talking to anyone or having great difficulty in sorting through her thoughts inside her head in order to speak, Melinda has a lot to say. Many of her thoughts reflect the alienation that she feels from her fellow students, her teachers, and her parents. For instance, she gives her least favorite teachers unflattering names. This name-calling makes Melinda's teachers a little less human in her mind. She can then create a bigger distance between them and her, which is what alienation is all about.

Melinda also creates a gap between herself and her fellow students. One way she does this is to put them down. In particular, she chooses the cheerleaders. She lumps the individuals together as a group and then tears into them. They all sleep with the football players, she states, and then come Monday morning they play their roles as goddesses. Melinda is obviously jealous of them, but rather than admit this human emotion, she alienates herself from them.

Melinda's parents are often not at home. When they are, Melinda rarely talks to them. Both parents are very busy and never seem to notice that Melinda is suffering. They know she is quiet and is not doing well in school, but they take that as a sign of disobedience rather than asking what is troubling her.

Suspense

Anderson does not reveal what is bothering her protagonist until well into the story. This creates suspense, which keeps her readers turning the pages to find out what is going to happen next and why Melinda is acting so strangely. Authors tend to use various forms of suspense to keep their readers engaged in the story. Suspense can also put readers in an active, rather than passive state, as they attempt to guess what happened by putting together the clues the author provides. Not all novels have to be classified as mysteries in order to create suspense. Most good novels have some element of suspense. Some are more subtle than others. Suspense is most obvious in crime novels and psychological thrillers. However, all well-written novels will provide enough unanswered questions to sustain the reader's curiosity and thus offer suspense.

Narrative Sequence

Throughout Anderson's novel, the narrative follows a certain path for only a short period. Rather than having long chapters devoted to a particular scene, Anderson hops from one short scene to another with little transition between them. This can be a little confusing at first, but by doing so, the author reflects the state of the protagonist's mind. Melinda admits that she has trouble sorting through her thoughts. For this reason, she has difficulty speaking. Her focus is on keeping her emotions buried, and this takes a lot of concentration. She sometimes loses control over her emotions and must run away. By jumping from one topic to another, the author recreates that same feeling in the reader's mind. For a few paragraphs, the reader follows the activities in Melinda's art class, for example. Then without any forewarning, Melinda might next be at home, in another class, or in the halls. The reader follows along, symbolically sharing the protagonist's unstable psychological state of mind, switching from one short thought to another.

Date Rape

According to the U.S. Department of Health and Human Services, the definition of *date rape* is when "forced sex occurs between two people who already know each other." Date rape occurs in about half of all rape cases reported. "Even if the two people know each other well, and even if they were intimate or had sex before, no one has the right to force a sexual act on another person against his or her will." The Department goes on to state that rape should not be confused with passion or love: "Rape is an act of aggression and violence." Another major point that the Department clarifies is that the victim of a rape should not feel that he or she brought it on by the clothes they were wearing or how they might have been acting: "Rape is always the fault of the rapist."

In a report offered by the U.S. Department of Justice, the number of incidents of date rape has slowly declined. In the 1990s, the time period for Anderson's novel, 1.1 million women reported intimate violence in 1993 as compared with 900,000 female victims in 1998. Of the female victims, women between the ages of sixteen and twenty-four were more likely to experience intimate violence than any other age group. The statistics for men, however, remained the same with about 160,000 violent crimes reported by an intimate partner both in 1993 and in 1998.

The Federal Government Source for Women's Health Information provides suggestions concerning how to avoid date rape and how to report an assault.

Development of the Young Adult Novel, 1960s to 2000s

Young Adult literature usually implies stories written for a teenage audience, roughly ninth through twelfth graders, though the age range can vary. Before the 1960s, Young Adult literature often meant romantic stories for girls and adventure books for boys. The material in Young Adult (YA) books rarely touched on controversial topics. Rather, the stories glossed over topics that were considered too involved with adult situations. However, with the 1960s, Young Adult literature began to change.

S. E. Hinton's novel, *The Outsiders* (1967), was one of the first to tackle teenage problems that had not previously been written about in literature for the young adult market. Hinton, only sixteen years old when she wrote the story, took on topics such as teen violence, drug and alcohol abuse, and dysfunctional family relationships. In the 1990s, the American Library Association (ALA) still listed this book as one of the most frequently challenged books by various adult groups wanting to ban the book from school libraries. Young Adult author Judy Blume raised eyebrows when she published her 1975 novel *Forever*, which included a discussion of teenage sex. Though the novel found its way into high school libraries, it too remains on the ALA's list of most challenged books. *The Chocolate War* (1974) by Robert Cormier is another Young Adult title that is often challenged because of its language and sexual content.

Despite the challenges some YA titles have received in the past, the popularity of novels both written for and read by teens has grown. According to Cecilia Goodnow, a writer for the *Seattle Post-Intelligencer*, not only are sales increasing but the quality of the material has significantly improved. The subject matter is becoming more sophisticated. For instance, one of the more popular teenage books is *The Book Thief* (2005) by Markus Zusak. This story is set in Nazi Germany and deals with the Holocaust.

Goodnow also points out that some of the most prestigious national book awards are reflecting the growing market as well as the improved quality of writing in the Young Adult field. In 1996, the National Book Foundation decided to include a Young Adult literature section to its considerations for annual awards. The ALA also expanded their annual awards to include the Michael L. Printz Award for Excellence in Young Adult Literature. *Speak* was named a Michael L. Printz Honor Book in 2000.

Critical Overview

Anderson's award-winning novel *Speak* attracted many teenage readers when it first came out in 1999, thus placing the novel on the *New York Times* best-seller list. Reviewers enjoyed the book as well. One critic, Casey Casias, writing for the *Santa Fe New Mexican*, states that *Speak* is a "truly enjoyable novel." Although Casias says books with depressing topics were not his usual fare, this one is "told with such dry wit and believable voice that it is impossible to put aside." Though the topic might be depressing, a reviewer for *Horn Book* calls the novel "an uncannily funny book" due to the witty observations that the protagonist uses. Debbie Carton, of *Booklist*, uses similar words to describe the novel. Carton writes that Melinda "recounts her past and present experiences in bitterly ironic, occasionally even amusing vignettes."

Another element that is often pointed out is the authenticity of the author's voice and her characters. Chris Liska Carger, writing for *Book Links*, refers to the "realistic picture" of high school that Anderson creates. A reviewer for *Publishers Weekly* points out Anderson's "gritty realism" and predicts that "Melinda's hard-won metamorphosis will leave readers touched and inspired."

What Do I Read Next?

- Anderson's novel *Catalyst* (2002) takes place at Merryweather High, the same setting in which *Speak* is set, but the focus in this novel is on different students. The novel's protagonist is Kate Malone, an honors student who pushes herself relentlessly to be her very best. Besides the good grades she makes, she runs cross country, takes care of her widower father and her brother, and works hard to stay out of trouble. When a neighbor's house burns down, she offers to share her bedroom with a teenager who once used to be her archenemy. These are not Kate's only challenges. She has applied to only one college, Massachusetts Institute of

Technology, a school with difficult admissions standards. As other students receive acceptance letters, Kate nervously waits to see if she made a big miscalculation.

- Anderson has received praise for her novel *Twisted* (2008), which focuses on the mental anguish of a teenage boy, Tyler Miller. Tyler was a computer nerd for most of his high school years. That is, until he pulled a graffiti prank that boosted his popularity but landed him a community service sentence doing physical labor all summer long. The punishment built his muscles as well as his character. When the new Tyler Miller enters his senior year, he is pleased with all the attention he receives, especially from Bethany Milbury. Tyler develops a big crush on Bethany, which infuriates her brother, Chip. Conflicts between Tyler and Chip keep the tension high at school, while fights with Tyler's alcoholic father provide anxious moments at home.

- Anderson's 2009 novel *Wintergirls* has received praise from several reviewers. The young protagonist, Lia, faces the problems of anorexia in what has been described as a very realistic portrayal. Anderson's writing skills makes this novel hard to put down despite the difficult topic of teenage self-destruction caused by a debilitating eating disorder.

- Melinda in Anderson's novel *Speak* finds solace in a janitor's closet at school, a place where she can hide. Keeping her company is a poster of author and poet Maya Angelou. Angelou is an African American writer who first came to fame through her book *I Know Why the Caged Bird Sings* (1970). Though written in the form of a novel, this book is actually the autobiography of Angelou's challenging childhood. The story is powerfully written and has become an inspiration for many teenage girls because of the strong emotions and courage that are displayed.

- *If I Stay* (2009) by Gayle Forman takes a different perspective on teenage life. In this story, the protagonist, Mia, has been in a car accident and is in a coma. As she lies in her hospital bed, her mind wanders back through her life, focusing on her relationships with her family and friends, with a special focus on her boyfriend. Should she fight to regain consciousness? In this novel, the protagonist digs down into her life to find the things that are most important to her.

- Sherman Alexie's *The Absolutely True Diary of a Part-Time Indian* (2007) is a story of the trials and tribulations of a tribal youth, Arnold Spirit, who tries to spread his wings. Arnold, known as Junior throughout most of the novel, is awkward in many different ways. Only his brain is perfectly coordinated. But when he decides to better his education by attending the public high school off-reservation, he finds trouble on both sides of the boundary lines. The story is told with humor, but the challenges Junior faces are emotional and trying.

Sources

Anderson, Laurie Halse, *Speak*, Farrar, Straus and Giroux, 1999.

Carger, Chris Liska, Review of *Speak*, in *Book Links*, January 2007, Vol. 16, No. 3, p. 38.

Carton, Debbie, Review of *Speak*, in *Booklist*, September 15, 1999, Vol. 96, No. 2, p. 247.

Casias, Casey, "Young Woman Finds Her Voice in *Speak*," in *Santa Fe New Mexican*, July 28, 2006, p. D3.

"The Federal Government Source for Women's Health Information," in U.S. Department of Health and Human Services Web site, http://www.womenshealth.gov/faq/date-rape-drugs.cfm (accessed April 25, 2009).

Goodnow, Cecilia, "Teens Buying Books at Fastest Rate in Decades—New 'Golden Age of Young Adult Literature' Declared," in *Seattle Post-Intelligencer*, March 7, 2007, http://www.seattlepi.com/books/306531_teenlit08.ht (accessed April 25, 2009).

Laurie Halse Anderson Home Page, http://www.writerlady.com/ (accessed April 25, 2009).

"The 100 Most Frequently Challenged Books of 1990-2000," in American Library Association Web site, http://www.ala.org/ala/issuesadvocacy/banned/frequ (accessed April 25, 2009).

Prince, Julie, "Writing from the Heart: An Interview with Laurie Halse Anderson," in *Teacher Librarian*, December 2008, Vol. 36, No. 2, pp. 70-1.

Rennison, Callie Marie, and Sarah Welchans, "Intimate Partner Violence," January 31, 2002, in U.S. Department of Justice Web site, http://www.ojp.usdoj.gov/bjs/pub/pdf/ipv.pdf (accessed April 25, 2009).

Review of *Speak*, in *Horn Book Magazine*, September 1999, Vol. 75, No. 5, p. 605.

Review of *Speak*, in *Publishers Weekly*, September 13, 1999, Vol. 246, No. 37, p. 85.

Further Reading

Covey, Sean, *The 6 Most Important Decisions You'll Ever Make: A Guide for Teens*, Fireside, 2006.

> Covey believes that teens have six very important decisions to make that will affect their entire future. He begins with the importance of a good education and continues through developing good relationships with parents, choosing whom to date, staying away from drugs, and developing self-confidence.

Ford, Amanda, *Be True to Your Self: A Daily Guide for Teenage Girls*, Conari Press, 2000.

> Written by a young author whose memories of teenage years were still fresh in her mind, Ford explores the challenges young girls face. She explores stories and advice about some of the most important issues facing young teenage girls, such as dating, drinking, self-esteem, relationships, dealing with parents, and building confidence.

Fox, Annie, *The Teen Survival Guide to Dating and Relating: Real-World Advice on Guys, Girls, Growing Up, and Getting Along*, Free Spirit

Publishing, 2005.

> Working from letters she received from teenagers, author Annie Fox gives advice about dating and relationships as well as about sexual identity and a sense of self.

Muhlberger, Richard, *What Makes a Picasso a Picasso?* Viking Juvenile, 1994.

> Picasso's cubist paintings helped open up new ways to look at objects (and helped protagonist Melinda, too). This book offers an introduction to the famed artist, exploring what he painted and why.

Nikkah, John, *Our Boys Speak: Adolescent Boys Write About Their Inner Lives*, St. Martin's Griffin, 2000.

> Nikkah was a graduate student in psychology when he gathered information from 600 teenage boys and wrote this book. Each chapter is a combination of the author's own recollections on the subject, followed by responses from the male teens. Topics range from sports to sex and include teenage angst, drugs, and death.

Simmons, Rachel, *Odd Girl Out: The Hidden Culture of Aggression in Girls*, Harcourt, 2003.

> Girls are often raised in a culture that

insists that they be nice. They should not express anger or acknowledge conflict. Instead, they turn to silence and passive aggression, the author concludes. After interviewing 300 girls, the author came up with specific acts, such as gossiping, note passing, and exclusion that young girls use to get back at someone they do not like. Simmons offers guidance and ways to increase better communication between girls and their friends and parents.

Warshaw, Robin, *I Never Called It Rape: The Ms. Report on Recognizing, Fighting, and Surviving Date and Acquaintance Rape*, Harper Paperbacks, 1994.

Writing for a young adult audience, a freelance journalist interviewed hundreds of male and female college students to put together his study of incidents of date rape. Warshaw also offers advice on how women can protect themselves and how men can avoid such situations.